How to Identify and Release Your Horse's Pain Points

An Owner's Guide

by

Lorrie Bracaloni C.H.P.

Lorrie Bracaloni does not diagnose, treat, or make medical claims in reference to equines. Releasing pain points and other methods described in this workbook and DVD are not a substitute for Veterinary care.

If your horse appears ill or lame, contact your Veterinarian immediately.

www.HappyNaturalHorse.com   e-mail@HappyNaturalHorse.com

Table of contents

Table of contents cont'd

Introduction

Before we begin, I want to thank you for learning how to help your horse be pain free.

I, Lorrie Bracaloni, became an equine naturopath health practitioner ten years ago. I was fortunate enough to study under some of the best holistic equine teachers in the United States. I love to educate horse owners on health and nutrition and have been for over ten years on the importance of natural, unprocessed, chemical-free nutrition for horses. My unique Equine Nutrition protocols and Herbal Remedies have helped hundreds of horses start down the road to excellent health and soundness.

I became very interested in natural care for my horses after my beloved horse, Romeo, died using conventional treatment. I have great respect for veterinarians. However my previous experiences with traditional veterinarians gave me very little information on the much-needed preventative care that I was looking for.

As a horse owner, I knew I was lacking crucial preventative care know-how, and caring for them in the conventional way just seemed to continually cost me money and time. My horses didn't seem to be as healthy as I thought they could be. After Romeo died of severe colic at the age of three, I swore I would learn all there was about natural horse care.

I attended a natural health seminar given by my horse trainer Brenda Flispe. Both my horse's and my life changed for the better. In that seminar, I discovered ways of helping my horses be more healthy and fit, and to prevent illness and injuries. It was at that seminar that I made it a point to learn and do all I could to reach out to the horse world, and pass on the knowledge I learned that day. My mentor, Dr. Regan Golob, showed me a whole new world of keeping my horse healthy and sound using natural feed and minerals. He also showed me the pain points on my horse and how to release them if they were out of balance. I continued attending many more seminars that Dr. Golob gave, and then went to school at the Holistic Therapies Center in Florida. There I received my Acupressure Certification from the Tallgrass Institute. Subsequently, I became certified in Animal B.E.S.T., Essential oils/ Raindrop therapy, Reiki Master level 3, herbal remedies, homeopathics, Equine Body Balancing Instruction, nutrition consulting, and Equine Chiropractic Application from Dr. Karmen.

I became amazed at the healing process once the body had been given the right nutrients and minerals coupled with applying the basic pain point balancing application on the horse when he is out of balance. My own horses have rarely seen a veterinarian in the last eight years. They are healthy and sound, much happier and calmer, and that has saved me money.

I have helped hundreds of horses over the past ten years. I rarely have to see the majority of my equine clients again because they resolve their health issues and stay healthy! Most of the clients I do see for yearly rechecks I find in good health and body balance. I have felt so blessed to be able to help so many horse owners find effective and natural health solutions for the horses they love, while saving them money.

This book is designed to help <u>you</u> help your horse when he is out of balance. It will help your horse become pain free. Anyone can learn this application. I also give hands-on workshops. Look me up on the web at www.happynaturalhorse.ws and www.naturalhorselb.ws.

<u>I suggest that you watch the DVD first, and then use the workbook for reference</u>.

What are Pain Points?

Most horse owners I meet tell me that I am their last resort. I often hear something like, "My horse has been scoped, x-rayed, massaged, had chiropractic adjustments and acupuncture, and even though all these things help, my horse is still off."

There is always a reason that a horse is sore. Mainly it has to do with how his muscles support his skeletal system. Muscles contract and release. When muscles tighten and cannot achieve a full release, they will remain tense and will shorten over time. This puts strain on the surrounding areas.

Because tightening and spasms are an extension of the normal contraction process, these types of problems do not show up on x-rays or standard testing procedures. The horse's problem can be a muscle misalignment.

Every move the horse makes produces stress upon a specific point. All muscles pull, so all skeletal motion is performed in this manner too. Tight muscles can lead to spasms, knots, muscle misalignment and blocked energy. When this happens you can start to see:

· Choppy strides
· Loss of impulsion
· Jump refusals
· Back soreness and hollowing
· Resistance to lateral flexion and bending
· Girthing problems
· Biting and other "bad behaviors"
· The horse being off and on "for no reason"
· Improper tracking forward, back, or laterally

Covering up minor problems most often ends up creating major ones.

Muscles are arranged in pairs of opposites, and muscles have two functions, to contract and release. In order for a muscle to release it must not have opposition and be able to stretch out. Muscle fibers attach to bone. So when muscles remain in a contracted state and are not released properly, this is where your horses **pain points** come in. The good news is, with this workbook, you can now learn how to release them just using your hands. When the pain points are released, then the muscles stop pulling on the bones, and the horse's natural balance can return. The pain can cease, and the muscle fibers can return to normal.

Did you know that 60% of your horse's body weight is skeletal muscle? Horses' muscles need oxygen and glucose from ingested food stuff. Oxygen is carried to the muscles by the circulation of blood. Any excess degree of muscle contraction or spasms will interfere with the free flow of oxygen into the muscle tissue and the outflow of toxins, which will have an effect on the horse's performance.

You now can check your horse's pain points before you ride him or when you are grooming him. By checking them you can prevent many problems before they develop. As Jack Meagher, Sports Therapist for people and equines alike said, "Remember any injury you can prevent is money in the bank!"

<u>You may find that releasing your horse's pain points</u>:
- Increases athletic performance and stamina
- Improves Muscle Tone
- Brings more become clearer and more responsive
- Enhances mental and emotional well being

When working on your horse, make sure it is not feeding time, and that he is not agitated or stressed.

You may use essential oils like Lavender or Release from Young Living to help relax him, or Flower Essences.

<u>I suggest that you watch the DVD first, and then use the workbook for reference</u>.

Atlas and Eyes — Checking

TO CHECK: To check the eyes, go to the front of your horse's head and hold his head straight, with his nose low so that you can see his eyes easily. Notice the top of each eye. You should be able to draw a straight line across the top of the eyes (Figure A). The eyes will look even if the atlas is even. Otherwise, the eye that is higher usually corresponds with the side where the atlas is higher (though the opposite was true for Dan in the video).

TO CHECK: To check the atlas alignment, hold your hand flat and place your palm downward just behind your horse's ears (Figure B). Run your flat hand from side to side. One side will feel higher than the other if it is misaligned. If that is the case, take note which side is higher.

Atlas and Eyes — Releasing

TO RELEASE: To release the horse's atlas and eyes, hold his tail firmly at the base of the tail (close to where it attaches to the body). Pinch or press on the horse's rear until he moves forward. Let the horse pull away from you while you hold his tail. Do not "pull" his tail. Hold for about one minute. Then slowly and gently let his tail go. Recheck his atlas to see if both sides are even.

Note: It can be helpful to have someone hold your horse for you and coax him forward as you hold his tail.

Tip: If you recheck the atlas and it has not changed, you can put some lavender oil on the atlas/poll area and try releasing again. You can also put drops of frankincense essential oil along the spine.

Note: A horse will be difficult to release if he is agitated (or acting up). You may have to wait until your horse is calmer.

Neck Pain Points — Checking

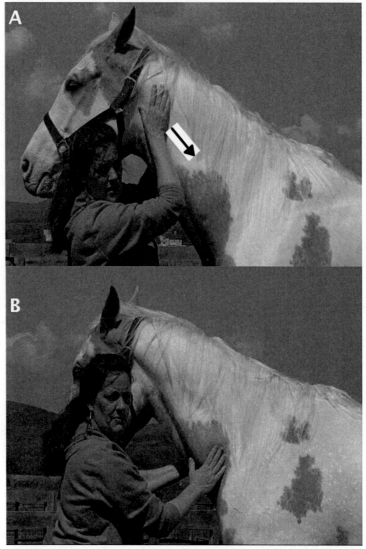

TO CHECK: Stand in front of your horse facing his chest. Hold both hands flat against his neck, starting up by his throat (Figure A), and move downward to the base of his neck (Figure B). As you are running your flat hand down each side of his neck, notice if you feel any unevenness, protrusions, or bumps. Take note of where they are. A bump usually means his muscles have locked around that vertebra, restricting movement.

Neck Pain Points — Releasing

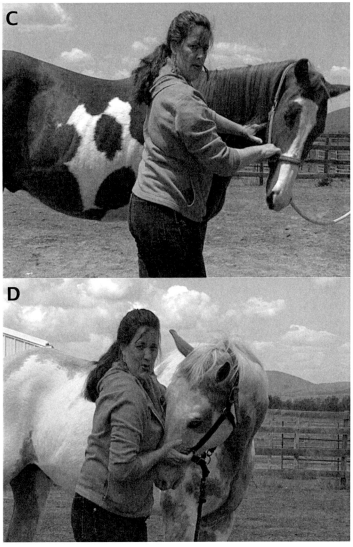

TO RELEASE: When working on the horse's right side, hold you left hand flat against the part of the neck that is protruding (Lorrie's left arm in Figure C). With your other hand, reach around to the left side of the horse's head, and bring his head around toward you, keeping his head as low as you can (Figure D). When you feel the resistance in the neck muscles, or when the horse stops or resists, gently let go of the horse's head. Let the horse take a breath and stretch out his neck on his own.

Then recheck the neck for bumps.

If the bump is still there, you can put lavender oil on the bump, and then try releasing the neck again. You can try to release this pain point up to 4 times, and the bump may go down a little bit each time. <u>Do not force the neck to go back into place</u>. Take the slow, gentle approach. This can be something that is done every day for a period of time. Opt for slow and steady progress.

As seen in the DVD, you can also do carrot stretches to help the horse's neck stay flexible. Take a carrot by the horse's nose, and guide his nose over to where his leg and body meet. Do this on both sides. You can also bring a carrot down to stretch his nose down by his knees, or lower towards his feet
(if he is able). This can be a nice way to keep your horse flexible and supple. Doing this once a week can help keep the horse's neck in place.

Note: A horse will be difficult to release if he is agitated (or acting up). You may have to wait until your horse is calmer.

Front Rib Pain Point — Checking

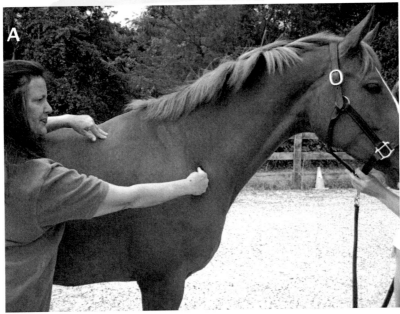

TO CHECK: Place your hand at the base of the withers* with your fingers pointing toward the ears, and your middle finger lying on top of the spine. Your thumb points down towards the ground. Where you thumb lies is the energy point. Now put your middle finger where you thumb is and "hold" that point. This hand holds the energy for checking the point (not every pain point requires this).

Then place your right hand in the groove where the neck and shoulder meet, and go to the middle of the groove. Press in here to feel how hard or soft the muscles are. If this area is hard (not soft and supple) it means that the muscles around the front rib are tight and constricted.

If there is tightness in this area, the horse may have a difficult time picking up either lead (depending on where else the horse is misaligned). The horse may also stomp a front leg more heavily than the other, be heavy on both feet, or be choppy in a gait.

*where the back comes into the withers

Front Rib Pain Point — Releasing

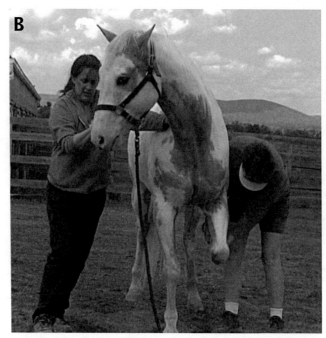

TO RELEASE: Get another person to pick up and hold the **left** front leg of the horse for you, as if they were going to clean out his foot (Figure B). Then holding the halter, bend the horse's head to the **right**. Keep his nose as low as possible as you do this. This is similar to what you do to release the neck pain points, however you are not bracing against the horse's neck, you are just bringing his neck around toward you. When you feel resistance, let go of the horse's head and foot as gently as you can. Sometimes this happens very quickly and the horse will pull his head and foot back from you. If that happens, do not resist the horse pulling away and let him go.

Give the horse a minute, see if he licks and chews, and then recheck the front rib area. See if it is softer. If it is still the same, you can try putting some lavender essential oil on the hard spot and try releasing again.

If it seems the horse's head will not go very far, DO NOT FORCE his head to go any farther than he will happily allow. Sometimes the front rib pain point will release by just turning the horse's head a little bit.

Check both sides of your horse!

Wither Pain Points — Checking

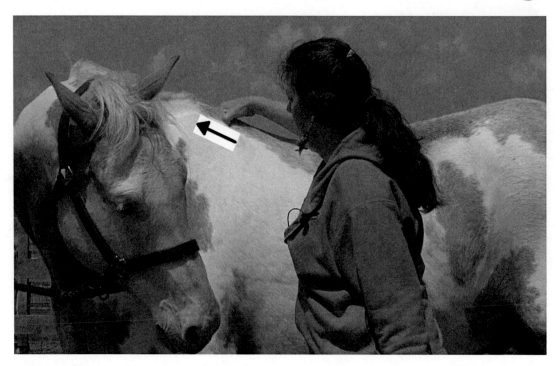

TO CHECK: Place your hand on the top of your horse's withers and open your hand so that your thumb is on one side of his withers, and the fingers are on the other. Pinch along both sides of the withers, moving up towards his neck. If the horse's withers react by flinching, the withers are misaligned. Some horses will actually buckle and their backs will drop down.

If the withers are misaligned, a horse may show his discomfort by rearing, bucking, biting, holding his head up high, "acting up," being "girthy," or being very uncomfortable to ride.

Wither Pain Points — Releasing

View of belly from below

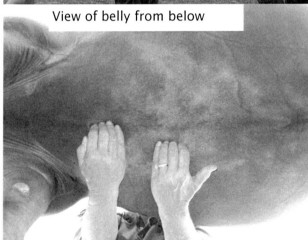

TO RELEASE: To release the pain points in the withers, place your hands underneath the horse's belly. Find the indentation in the middle of his belly that is directly below the spine. Then move your fingers along that indentation until you are directly below the withers. Bend your fingers and push your fingernails up into the belly, and use your leg muscles to push the horse's belly upward. LOOK UP towards the horse's back as you do this. The horse should lift his back. Hold his back up for about thirty seconds if you can. back come down again and and remove your hands. Let the horse breathe, and recheck the withers.

Tips: 1. Remember to look up!

2. If your horse's back does not lift up, you can try using rocks to push into his belly instead of your fingernails. Slowly increase the pressure until you get his back to lift.

3. It can be helpful to have someone hold your horse when you do this to keep him from moving away.

Girth Pain Points — Checking

TO CHECK: To check the girth pain points, poke your finger behind the horse's front leg, about four inches up from the bottom of the belly. Poke left, right, up and down in this general area and see if the horse flinches or if he seems indifferent to your poking.

Girth Pain Points — Releasing

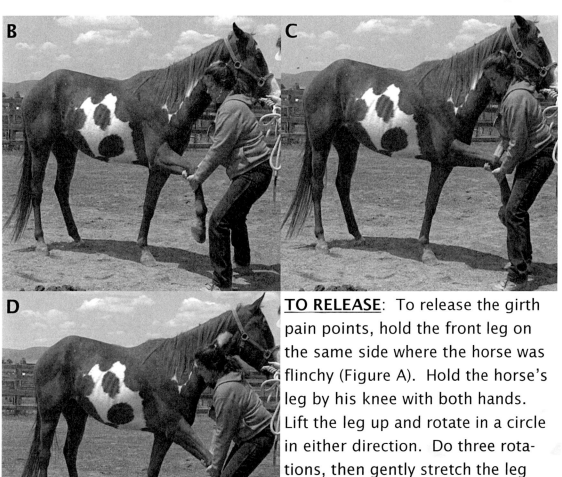

TO RELEASE: To release the girth pain points, hold the front leg on the same side where the horse was flinchy (Figure A). Hold the horse's leg by his knee with both hands. Lift the leg up and rotate in a circle in either direction. Do three rotations, then gently stretch the leg down and place it on the ground (Figure D).

Sometimes the horse will stretch his leg and place it down himself. Allow him to do that while you support his leg. Release your hold when he places his foot on the ground. Stand back and let the horse breathe and lick and chew. Then recheck the girth pain points. If the horse is flinchy on both sides, do this release on both sides of the horse.

Back Rib Pain Points — Checking

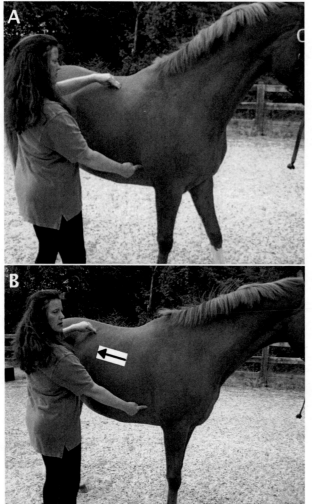

TO CHECK: When on the horse's right side, first take your right hand and place a finger in the girth area as shown in Figure A (this holds the energy for checking these pain points). Keep your right hand there and press along the top of the skeletal ribs with your other hand (see skeletal drawing Figure C). Start pressing just behind the withers, and keep pressing along to the end of the ribcage (Figures B and C). If the horse flinches or buckles when you do this, then his muscles are sore and the back rib at that location is misaligned. Take note of the spot or spots where the horse's back twitched.

Remember to check both sides of your horse.

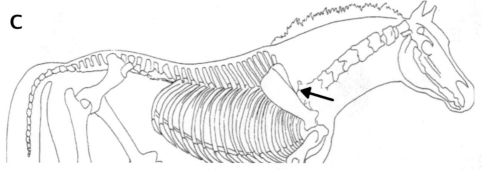

Back Rib Pain Points — Releasing

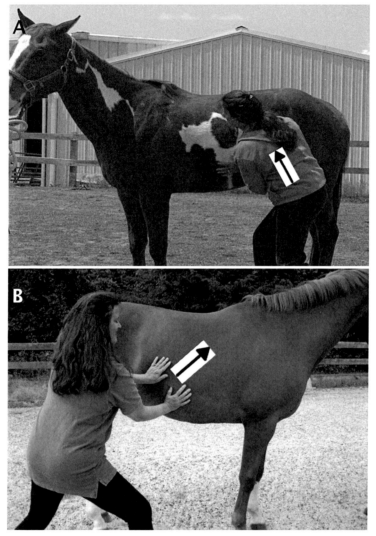

TO RELEASE: To release the back rib pain points you will place both hands on the horse with thumbs towards each other (see Lorrie's hand position in Figure B). Position your hands in this manner together under the ribcage and push up slightly but firmly <u>TOWARDS THE WITHERS</u>, NOT STRAIGHT UP OR TOWARDS THE BUTT. LOOK UP towards the back as you do this. The push is a quick motion. Just push and release.

Let the horse breathe, lick and chew, and recheck.

Stifle Reflex Point — Checking

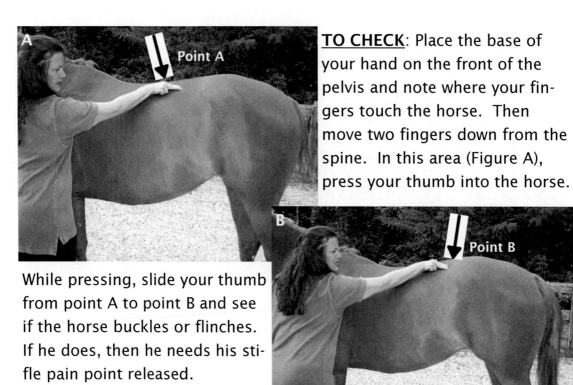

TO CHECK: Place the base of your hand on the front of the pelvis and note where your fingers touch the horse. Then move two fingers down from the spine. In this area (Figure A), press your thumb into the horse.

While pressing, slide your thumb from point A to point B and see if the horse buckles or flinches. If he does, then he needs his stifle pain point released.

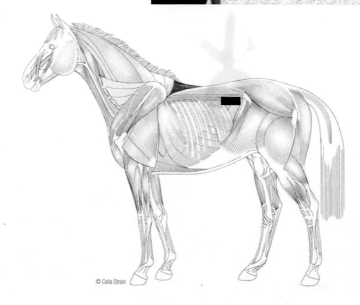

© Celia Strain

Stifle Reflex Point — Releasing

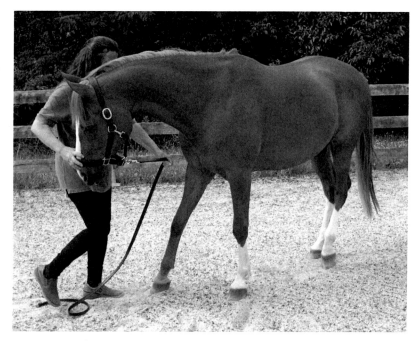

TO RELEASE: To release the stifle pain point, keep the horse's head low as you push the horse back quickly (not in slow motion). There has to be a good pace backward, keeping the head down. Move the horse backward at least 8 to 10 steps. While you are doing this, have the intention of helping to release the left stifle or right stifle, whichever you just checked.

Recheck the stifle pain point. Check both sides. If the horse still reacts (buckles or flinches), repeat the backward stepping up to three more times. You can also move on to check and realign the hip area, (next page) and then recheck the stifle pain points again.

Note: You can check the stifle on one side, get the horse to step backwards, recheck and find the pain point is no longer painful. Then when you go to check the other side of the horse, you may find that pain point also needs released. This may seem strange, because it would seem

seem that backing up the horse should release both stifle pain points. Your focus and intention can make a difference. When you back up the horse, have the intention to release the stifle you just checked. Or, you can try having the intention of releasing both stifles, recheck, and see what happens.

Hip Alignment — Checking

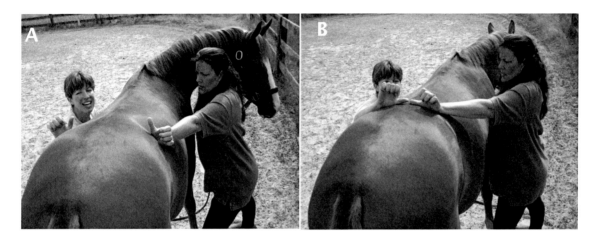

There are two ways to find if the hip bones are aligned:

1. You can check the hip alignment by having two people stand on each side of the horse. Each person places their hand in front of the pelvic bone and point their fingers toward the spine (Figure A). Send your hands toward the spine to see if they meet. If they do not meet at the spine, the hips are misaligned. You can see in Figure B that Lorrie and Becky's thumbs do meet, so the horse's hips are aligned.

2. You can also stand behind the horse as shown below, using a mounting block if needed for a better view. Because you are behind the horse you could get kicked, so consider your safety. Place your hands just in front of the pelvic/hip bone (Fig. C) and bring them together at the top of the spine. See if the thumbs line up or do not. They do not line up in Fig. D, so in this example the horse does need her hips released. In Fig. E her thumbs come together so the horse's hips are fine.

Hips Alignment — Releasing

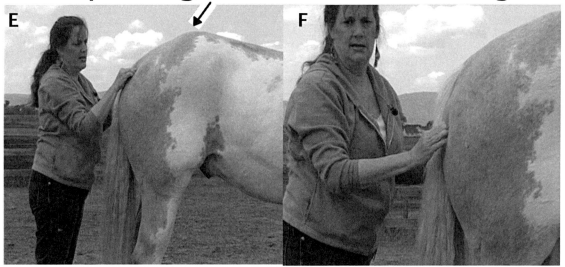

TO RELEASE: Point and press your fingernails into the horse on either side of the tail. Start at the top of the croup (arrow in Figure E), and keep pressing as you go down to the middle of the horse's hind end (Figure F). Push in as you go down, and then push in more and hold when you get to the place shown in Figure F. Hold for the count of five or more. If horse moves while you are doing this, then start again and hold it as long as you can. It can be helpful to have someone holding your horse to keep him from moving.

Recheck the pelvis/hip alignment. You can try this "butt tuck" again if the hips are still out of alignment.

I recommend you do this as part of your preventative care (before you ride) at least once a week.

Tip: If the horse is not responsive, use tools! Instead of your fingernails, use little rocks or a hard brush. You don't want to hurt the horse, just get him to lift his back and tuck his hind end. Some horses are more sensitive to pressure than others.

Hock Pain Points — Checking

The inner hock point is located in the middle of the hindquarters along the groove edge of the prominent muscle groove (at the edge of the semitendinosus muscle - see arrows in Figure A). Go to the middle of that groove (middle meaning between the top and bottom of the horse's hind end), and place your fingers here. This is the pain point for the inner hock. Then open your hand and place your thumb on the horse (towards the stifle, not towards the tail - See Figure B). This is the outer hock point. Check one at a time, by pressing the point with five pounds of pressure. See if the horse reacts by stepping away in pain, or twitching his muscles in that spot. Check inside hock, outside hock point, and then check both together at the same time.

If both spots are reactive, that shows that the horse may need to see the equine dentist, or that the teeth have been recently floated.

Hock Pain Points — Releasing

<u>TO RELEASE:</u> If your horse is reactive to just one of the hock points on one left side or the right side, then there may be an injury to the outside (lateral) hock, or the inside (medial) hock. You can check the hock to see if it is warm to the touch. The horse may need Veterinary attention and an x-ray. There is no specific pain point release for this.

I was demonstrating at a Richard Shrake clinic, and one horse kept buckling when I pushed on the outside hock point. We checked the hock joint, and on the outside was a fresh cut from the horse being kicked. Richard was amazed!

Hunter's bump

A hunter's bump is an indentation just in front of the pelvis (this horse doesn't have it, but Durango in the DVD does. The horse at the bottom of the page does as well.

HUNTER'S BUMP EXERCISE: Bring your hands four fingers back from the front edge of the pelvis, and then come out laterally four fingers from the spine on both sides. Push in to the horse here, and the hunter's bump will lift upwards.   Hold for one minute.

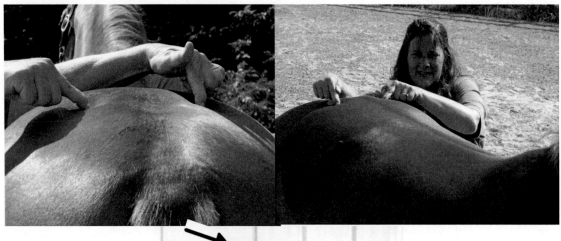

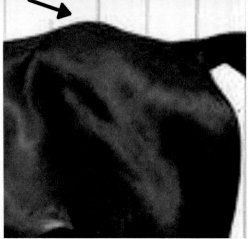

Hunter's Bump (picture from www.jwequine.com)

If Your Horse Does Not Hold His Pain Point Releases

Every function in the body requires a mineral!

"You can trace EVERY sickness... and EVERY ailment to a mineral deficiency"
Dr. Linus Pauling,
Nobel Prize-Winning Scientist

 A misalignment has another component in pain. The reason is found in this excerpt from a Pete Ramey article:

Copper supports enzymes that form the strengthening cross-links between collagen and elastin molecules in connective tissue. Deficiencies lead to abnormalities in bone, cartilage, tendons, ligaments, and arterial walls among the most dramatic consequences. In horses, copper deficiency has been linked to uterine artery rupture in mares, a fatal complication of labor. Copper deficiency is known to cause developmental bone disease in foals. From research in other animals we also know that copper deficiency has adverse effects in hair quality. Although it hasn't been studied in horses, remember that the ingredients and growth mechanisms for hair and the hoof are virtually identical.

Zinc performs a host of functions in the body. Structures on proteins called zinc fingers allow them to bind to DNA. Zinc fingers also influence the folding and structure of proteins. In enzyme systems, zinc is essential for pigment formation, antioxidant function, transport of carbon dioxide in the blood, bone building and remodeling, insulin production and release among others. IEleanor Kellon, VMD]

Now I knew I had found the tip of an iceberg; I enrolled in Dr. Kellon's basic course "NRC Plus" www.drkellon.com. I firmly believe that every person responsible for taking care of horses should take this online course. It will teach you the relationships, roles and importance of vitamin labels, forage analysis and teaches you how to really provide for your horses' needs.

During this course, when I looked back at my pasture and hay analysis from the past, it became clear that the lack of copper and zinc were the least of my problems. In my area, the grass, hay, water (and even the mineral blocks I was recommending) consistently have extremely high levels of iron. *[Excess iron cancels the absorption of copper and zinc- even if there is an "adequate" amount of those minerals available. Excess iron has many effects, including predisposition to infection, a predisposition to arthritis and increased risk of tendon/ligament problems, liver disease and altered glucose metabolism – including insulin resistance and overt diabetes. Eleanor Kellon, VMD]* High body iron levels drive insulin resistance, and vice versa. This may explain why the high sugar content of the grass had an exaggerated effect on the horses living on the high-iron pastures and water sources. I was first called to each of these facilities because of acute and/or chronic laminitis, and the problems persisted even with grazing muzzles or dirt paddocks with hay (from the same region). Now I understand why.

The most frustrating part is that after taking that class, I can now read the labels on equine feeds and supplements and compare them to the horses' actual needs. The deception is sinful. Horse owners buy a supplement and/or commercial feed and think they have covered all the bases of nutrition. They read the label and see, "It's in there": Zinc, copper, biotin, calcium, phosphorus.... All the things they are told their horse needs for optimal health and performance listed in ppm (parts per million) or percentages, but they don't know what it means. They put their faith in the manufacturer. In most cases, the actual levels provided are only a fraction of what the horse needs.

One very popular daily supplement I found at a customer's barn was 93% salt and had 3ppm of zinc proudly printed on the label. Since zinc was listed (along with a dozen other minerals in similar amounts) the owner thought she had the trace minerals covered. Her 880 pound horse would actually have to eat 220 pounds of this supplement per day to get the <u>minimum</u> NRC requirement for zinc! (Needless to say this would kill the horse.) Deception- and our horses are suffering for it.

To make matters worse, if a supplement does not complement the grass, hay and other feeds it is worthless or even toxic. Understand this all varies- every pasture and hay field has a unique mineral profile and will thus have unique supplement needs. You should test each of your horses' food sources and consider the entire nutrition profile together. The horses with little or no access to green grass are subject to the same problems as well- it all depends on the soil in the hay field. Additionally, the hay-drying process eliminates vitamin E and essential fatty acids so important for skin (hooves) and for fighting inflammation. These must be supplemented if the horse has limited access to green stuff.

At boarding facilities, where hay and grains provide most of the calories, I'm seeing another very common scenario. The horses are often getting too much calcium and not enough phosphorus. It is important that they are balanced in a 2:1 ratio respectively. Alfalfa and in some areas even grass hays tend to have a ratio of 5+ :1. This creates a functional lack of phosphorus that can lead to angular deformities in foals and bone loss in older horses. This does not mean that you should blindly supplement phosphorus. Too much phosphorus also robs the horse of calcium. You must test the forage!

Excess calcium could also make magnesium less available to the horse. *[The symptoms of inadequate magnesium are the same as those of excessive ionized calcium. These include irritability, hypersensitivity, muscular symptoms from twitching to spasm, with a potential for GI symptoms and heart irregularity when severe. Horses with moderate magnesium deficiency are often misdiagnosed as EPSM. Other magnesium responsive clinical symptoms I have seen are gait disturbances, including stilted gait, base wide gait behind, difficulty controlling the hind end. horse is not a happy camper! Eleanor Kellon, VMD]*

Salt is another very common deficiency I see everywhere I go. Most horse owners think that if they provide a salt block, the horses' sodium needs are met. In truth, horses do not receive adequate levels of sodium by licking a salt block. One sedentary horse would have to consume over 2 pounds (an entire stall sized brick) in one month. If he was working, he might need 2-4 times more than that. Salt is ideally provided in a loose form. Most horse owners don't realize how critical it is for their horse's sodium needs to be met. [*Sodium is essential for absorption of many nutrients, as well as their entry into cells (**including glucose**), essential for the normal functioning of all nerve and muscle tissue. Sodium is also the major regulator of water balance in tissues. In addition to "holding" water in the tissues, sodium is what the brain "reads" in determining when to trigger thirst and when to regulate the amount of sodium, and therefore water, the body excretes in the urine. If sodium intake is too low, the kidneys will actively excrete potassium and save sodium, even if blood potassium levels drop below normal. This is a very, very common mistake made when supplementing performance horses.*

Insufficient sodium inevitably leads to some dehydration. The brain reads sodium levels in the cerebrospinal fluid. The cerebrospinal fluid in turn is a filtrate of blood. Blood levels of sodium will be maintained by "stealing" sodium from the extracellular fluid. This leads to the decrease in skin elasticity that is familiar sign of mild to moderate dehydration. The rule of thumb is that as little as 2 to 3% dehydration can lead to a 10% drop in performance. However, excessive intakes need to be avoided. Eleanor Kellon. VMD] Again, actually testing and supplementing specific amounts is optimum.

These are only a few small examples of <u>many</u>. Horses need to consume each nutrient in adequate amounts and usually in balance with the amounts of several other nutrients. This is not just about growing healthy hooves, either. Balanced nutrition profoundly effects attitude, immune function, strength, endurance, recovery; actually every aspect of health and performance. If your horses are having problems of any kind, you can bet there is a nutritional component. So far, every time I have had troubles growing healthy feet and have tested the forage, I have found significant mineral ratio problems and/or deficiency- every time. The nutrition balance may be all or part of your horse's problem, whether you are concerned about a training issue, recovery from an illness or carving 2/10 of a second off your lap time.

The best news is that feed testing, balancing and supplementation saves most horse owners a considerable amount of money (Now why haven't the feed companies told us about this?). but you will be required to think, rather than just blindly throwing your money away. When I tested the grass and hay in my area, along with the bad news [no Zn or Cu] I got some great news: The grass was completely covering **ALL** of the other nutritional needs- my customers with pasture can meet NRC guidelines of every nutrient (including protein) for pennies a day. Too many horse owners spend hundreds of dollars a month to keep their horses constantly on the brink of laminitis by feeding buckets of feed and random supplements "just in case" the horse is missing something in his diet. Why not find out exactly what he is missing and just buy that?

Here's how to do it:

> Take samples of your hay and grass. Send them in for testing to www.equi-analytical.com (read the directions for sampling on that site). Your analysis will be emailed to you in a few days. Choose the 601 package for $35 as a start for most situations (a more comprehensive package is available for $79)

(This is an excerpt from Pete Ramey's article. If you would like to continue reading, you can find the rest at: http://www.hoofrehab.com/diet.htm)

The reason why your horse doesn't hold his pain point releases usually has to do with mineral imbalances, so it is important that you know what you are feeding. Read your labels, get your feed analyzed, and observe your horse. Recently I have found a really good mineral that covers all the horse's nutritional needs. It is called Highland's Big Sky. You can order by calling 330-893-2016. He ships it from Ohio.

If your horse's pain point releases are not holding, or if you are having a difficult time with the concepts presented in the workbook and DVD, you can contact me for a consultation.

www.happynaturalhorse.com

Acknowledgements

A special thank you to Erika Trexler for making this possible and believing in me, doing the video, editing, and helping put the workbook together. And thank you to our husbands for supporting us and this project.

Thank you to Julie Bolton for helping us with the DVD, and letting us film at your farm, and for assisting us with your horses Dan and Durango.

Thank you to Joe Osmann, Richard Schellenburg, and Jason Santelli of the FCC Video Program for your video assistance.

Reference Bibliography

Zidonis, Nancy & Snow, Amy & Soderberg, Marie, *Equine Acupressure: A Working Manual. A Hands-On Approach To Your Horse's Well-Being.* Tallgrass Publishers, LLC, 90-859-69. Page 108.

Pete Ramey: http://www.hoofrehab.com/diet.htm

Ceila Strain, illustration, page 18.

Recommended Books, and websites

My mentor, Dr. Golob: www.DocGolob.com

My mentor, Julie Montgomery, N.D.: www.dragonflyfarms.com

For more information about Equine Body Balancing, and Animal B.E.S.T. go to this site: http://www.morter.com/animalbest/

Pete Ramey's website: www.hoofrehab.com

To get an analysis of your hay and grain: http://www.equi-analytical.com/CommonFeedProfiles/disclaimer.asp

To see maps of your local area, pasture, and heavy metal readings in your area: http://tin.er.usgs.gov/geochem/doc/averages/countydata.htm

For natural remedies: http://www.homeopathyworks.com/jshop/

For more about connecting with and understanding your horse's behavior: Carolyn Resnick: http://www.dancewithhorses.com/index.html

Equine Acupressure: A Working Manual. A Hands-On Approach To Your Horse's Well-Being. Tallgrass Publishers, LLC

About the Author

Lorrie Bracaloni is a Certified Holistic Practitioner (C.H.P.) who became certified in the following fields of equine health:

- Nutrition
- Acupressure (Tallgrass Institute)
- Animal B.E.S.T.
- Herbal Remedies
- Homeopathics
- Reflexology
- Essential Oils and Young Living Raindrop Application
- Dr. Karmon, DC. Chiropractic Applications
- Reiki Master, Level 3

For over ten years, Lorrie has also studied and practiced stress point applications by Jack Meagher, EFT, Applied Kinesiology i.e. muscle testing, and "The Work" of Katie Byron.

Lorrie also teaches and gives demonstrations and clinics on reflexology and releasing your horse's pain points. She is currently writing a book on the most prominent reasons equine veterinarians are called for emergencies, and what to do while waiting for the veterinarian to arrive, as well as for preventative care. Lorrie also works with people on living their most abundant life.

Upcoming Books and DVDs by Lorrie Bracaloni, C.H.P.

The Top Seven Reasons for Emergency Equine Veterinarian Calls. What To Do While You Wait, and Ways to Prevent These Emergencies. A Holistic Guide.

Health 101, Nutrition For Your Horse

Made in the USA
Middletown, DE
07 November 2014